VICIOUS DOGS ATTACK ME IN SLEEPLESS NIGHTS OF SUMMER

a collection of prose, tales, and streams of semi-consciousness

by Scott H. Schiaffo

editor Mary Anne Christiano-Mistretta **book design illustrations and layout** by Scott Meaney **production assistant** Christopher Laudando **photos** Tom Zanca **legal** Joseph R. McClure Esq.

special thanks:
Special thanks to Carrie Werner, Michael P. Russin,
Tom Zanca, Frank Saccomanno,
Mary Anne Christiano-Mistretta, Christopher Laudando, Scott
Meaney, Paula R. Danzinger, Ph.D., LPC, CCMHC,
Kevin Smith, Scott Mosier, all at View Askew, and Jay & Silent Bob's
Secret Stash, all of my Facebook friends and last
but not least all of the "Clerks" fans around the world!

a letter from the author

Dear reader:

Take a journey with me; back to the early 90s – back to a time when my addictions ran the entire show. I was up to my neck in alcoholism and drug addiction.

During this period of my life, my reputation as a rogue actor enabled me to develop an offbeat career in the independent film & music industry. As they say, "God watches over drunks and small children." It was during my descent into an alcoholic/drug addiction abyss, I had auditioned for a film called "Clerks." In between desperate blackouts, ODs, and trips to the emergency room, I managed to give a spirited performance in Mr. Smith's audacious debut film. Kevin was pleased with me, and I was ecstatic that I didn't muck it up or blow it by binging myself into the emergency room before he shot my scenes.

One week prior to the premiere of "Clerks" I landed in an Intensive Care Unit in Pennsylvania. This unfortunate incident was the result of a binge that started six days earlier on the Lower East Side. As I regained consciousness, a priest was hovering over my bed holding a bible in his hand. As he made the sign of the cross, he recited my last rites: "Yea, though I walk through the valley of the shadow of death, I will fear no evil: for thou art with me; thy rod and thy staff they comfort me."

Needless to say, I never made it to the Clerks premiere.

It was during this time I felt oddly compelled to document my downward spiral into hell by writing funky prose, tales, and streams of semi – consciousness.

Strap yourself in, it's a bumpy ride to say the least!

Scott Schiaffo - 2012

Mary Anne Christiano-Mistretta

I'll never forget meeting Scott for the first time, a cool, laid-back, actor musician, who was to write music to my poetics on a music/poetry compilation called: "See It, Feel It Hear It Vol. 1" which was published in a cassette series back in the early 1990s.

Scott's guitar style, which resembled Johnny Thunders a bit, was extremely complimentary to my off-beat street styled poetry and more than 20 years later, our work together still passes the test of time.

After creating together professionally, Scott and I became buddies. We had the same taste in music. Barely 30-years-old, we were both young and full of piss and vinegar. We spent a lot of time hanging out in nightclubs. The punk scene was long gone, but we had a mutual admiration for a band called D-Generation and followed them around NYC and New Jersey.

It was during this time that Scott had a role in Kevin Smith's debut classic, "Clerks". Scott had it all going for him and had the world by the balls. He seemed to be an up and rising star as he was being interviewed in all the coolest music magazines and newspapers in New York and New Jersey at the time.

During this time, Scott told me that a former MTV VJ wanted to go to the Clerks premiere with him, but he wanted to go with me instead – and I was both honored and thrilled!

We never made it to the premiere. This is when I started to realize Scott wasn't drinking just for fun – Scott had a serious problem. Our outings to shows stopped and instead our friendship was late night drunken phone calls.

One of my saddest memories I have of Scott was my last visit with him before we became estranged. We were going to meet at his place. When I got to Scott's house, he was waiting for me outside. I didn't recognize him. In just a few weeks time, he went from a handsome actor – who was my friend – to a bloated and dispirited stranger that I almost didn't recognize. It wasn't even noon and he was already extremely drunk. The sun was out and it was a most gorgeous day, but Scott wanted all the shades down. I was sad and scared for him.

That was the last time I saw Scott – for a very, very long time; that being said dear readers, this collection of poetry written by Scott Schiaffo is the real deal. Or shall I say, was the real deal, as I'm happy to say that Scott has long recovered from his serious addictions. We reconnected a few years back and I'm ecstatic to be working with him once again.

Mary Anne Christiano-Mistretta 2012

VDAMISNOS

symphony of streets

what gorgeous music the streets make
cars, sirens, people, bottles clank, dogs and cats
wailing car radios pass and fade into the night
all of this in-between thoughts of you and
where you are tonight

tonight i blend
drink and grin at this life
how i truly love the streets and their inhabitants
we all come and go like children bursting out
and scattering around the playground
if only the charade could be captured
frozen
studied

we may find an answer and stop running
but not tonight
just a wonderful street symphony plays
i'll always be a fan
play on and on
extend the night
beat daylight with encores of glorious
sounds of night

hotel room rot

at the end of the line
i sit in my $40 a night room
surrounded by ghosts of past hotel dwellers
the stench of sex, smoke and booze lingers
alone, in silence, i swig and die a little inside
with each day comes a new game

today, i lose

two bags deep

tinkle your umbrella folds across my hairy chest
more drink and no hospitals is today's chant
work your bitter heart into a frenzy of the forgotten
playing the music loud to everyone's displeasure

all this comes and goes like changing reflections
mirrors do lie
so do pictures and drunks
what you need is never what you get
isn't it too bad we all can't die on cue

rub eyes and forehead in one motion and wish you were
two bags deep

vicious dogs attack me
in sleepless nights of summer

where is the spark?
void of any passion
i exist
i have never lived
standing at a crossroads
i don't want to move in any direction
wishing the earth would open up its soil and drown me in dirt
drown me in words
drown me in folly
wanting the bottle more than any of this
hating all
being vacant
my head wails in lament for lack of escape and originality
voices always talking
never listen
my life hurts
never sleeping
waking in pain and fear of the sun, another day, bottles, no
bottles, people, love, money, cars, women, family, eternity in this
empty shell, ghosts of past sin, my father, music, films, television,
reading, talking, making sense of the senseless, plugging onward
into a spiral swirl of blood red lovers death
feeling truly mad
laugh at myself and sharp tongue
verbal slaughter for the world around me
obsessed with music, the written word and photographs
no heroes here
vicious dogs attack me in sleepless nights of summer
hating the sun
praying and moaning for any kind of reprieve
it will never come
only death
and death has a busy schedule

sparkle the girl

she shines, sparkle the girl
giggles, bubbles and the moon are hers
she tells the sun to shine

sparkle fills my void and does not know
floating on air, I want to always breathe her in
like the night she is everywhere

she had given me more than she can know,
her gift won't fade
unlike jaded lovers and friends
I pray i will always have her sparkle in my veins

we drink the night like parched baby death

vanity kills
vanity spins me silly
package over contents
i'm drowning quickly for such a shallow man
all the time wanting solace
achieving only desperate blackouts

god watches over drunks and children
the desperate have only the night and it's blackness
we drink the night like parched baby death
silent screams of vanity

mirrors blare the truth like hell's trumpets
vain angels and their surprise
you have the need but not the strength
this too will pass
you will live to see yet another sun
this is utter folly

bing

bing
drunk, beats his kids
bill holden's head against the coffee table

me
jumped, robbed, beaten and left in a hallway in
harlem
and you
living with someone

the longest day of the year

sit still in silence
the clock ticks away my life and decision
hating all that I have become
but loving all the madness

herbal tea and a bad bag of reefer
what a shitty breakfast
tic tic tock tock

the typer just hums through the silence
it's a cycle i'm told
let it finish its course

cluster fuck

i am not
bald, fat, a junkie, drunk, stoned, high, horny, happy,
content, smiling, rich, poor, free, enslaved, dirty,
clean, or dead

i am, however
bored, uninspired, lifeless, and completely void

creed

inconsistency is the death of discipline
discipline brings true freedom
i have been chained to excess for as long as i can remember
pain and pleasure rule our every thought
i don't want to feel anymore

booze and drugs once liberated me
now they keep me in my place
i don't even care
just say "no"

or just say "yes" to being numb and mindless
my mind is not correct
now i play the chicken and the egg game
was i ever correct?
or am i one of the lost?

most of the time i believe in me
maybe that's better odds than most are given
or maybe nothing really matters much
this is what i suspect to be the real case

scene

who needs that shit from a crazy lady?
not me
well, maybe me
yeah, me
lucky to be out of there
no fucking little blue christs
no 911
give me love or give me death
I'll take death

wow!

morning beer
it is a good thing i don't smoke
hell is in my mouth,
endless cycle of wanton
slim as Christ on the pole for my sins

i think not therefore i am dying
nose bleeds, heroin dreams
woman in teddy, haunting images of debtors
love is the strange beast

give me all the pains and pangs
I will handle

naked

clothed in words
layer around layer
life deep in truth and circumstances
life is about constant movement
we ease through the minutes of the day
sometimes with little grace
perhaps only to continue to pass away

i know little about the folly of guilt
punching bag,

charity care motherfucker that i am
today i am alive

writing, playing, eating sparks
all in a day's time

crap it out

eat something bad
relax, you will crap it out
food, junk, booze, or dope will always come out of you
not life though
that stays in and gets deeper

spent

27 and spent
my body a mass of beaten flesh
bloody nerves in a frenzy
three fingers crippled by the bottle and the written word
sinking in a sea of clinics and doctors

amassing pain and regret with every passing breath
please
suck the pain
hate
hurt
fear
from my gut
is this what becomes of the bent?

running, never arriving anywhere that looks like life
let me vomit all the hell out
wipe me clean
Christ take me
with a blink of an eye, i'll be spent

toodles

sun and shine
ray of hope

faith a lifeline
grab the rope

bury me
spilling doubt
in blood red sea

take a step
never fails
another step
county jails

the sick in the street
wars at home
flesh is meat
always alone

never smile
burn inside
putrid vile
can not hide

from what i am, and what
i'll never be

stitch

he lay on the ground
lifeless at peace

all that was heard was a loud smack
it rang through the apartments into
the still night air
the night just hung

the ones around him were angry on the outside
crushed on the inside
he was failing himself, it didn't seem to matter
this was the real dilemma, life or death held
little importance

he peeled himself off the pavement
his chin began to distill blood onto his front

without hesitation, he leaped for another drink
the police would be here soon to stop the madness
at least for this evening

"why is he doing this?" they all ask
fighting life choosing slow death
liquid death
powders
tobaccos
circumstance

void of any real explanation they all hung their heads
at least we'll all sleep tonight
stripped of his dignity
raped by his own excesses
charged with being a condemned soul
they took him away

to be fixed
mended
stitched

it's everything all at once

still dancing on the planet
holidays leave me empty
i am never complete
alone but never lonely, why?

everything makes perfect sense in chaos
like twisted melody through a bent harmony

it leaves satisfied, but not for very long
i once saw the world as black and white

now i am drowning in gray

all the drunks in the world and me

a sorry lot we are
drinking
pissing
yelling
swearing
screaming (sometimes silently)
hating
hurting
praying
and one day closer to the end

trapped

business men
business lunches
talking shop
talking about the family

barbecues on Sunday
anniversaries
weddings
tonsils out
graduations
funerals
dinner parties
divorce
mortgage
two cars
a good book
some television
occasional cinema
theater
adultery
promotions
holiday shopping
bedtime story
vacations
and ultimately...
death

i am guaranteed at least one of these

the perfect season

ice cream cocks on lovers lane
strong willed handsome irishmen

gorgeous spaniard women
stiletto night into cold wet mourning

the sage can see the misgivings of the masses
the fool plays his part with bravado

we die with the grace of cats in the wind
blowing us to the end

the desperate fear life more than death
death seems sweet

death doesn't come
it waits for a cue
silence is welcome
bittersweet fruit-child

lay in the mud
she has a keen sense of reason
the perfect season

dr. john
for Dr. John Popowich

he will do fine
he has the passion for life and survival
i lost him to the spines
but it's o.k.
the spines need him
fuck it
we all can't drown

christ on my keychain

so it's back to my bottle and words
let this edge break my moral fabric
people say writing is easy
you just sit behind the typer and open up your wrists

splendid!

the madness has just begun and i am already empty

gray tones where are you?

you

you
walking away from me in your underwear
thumbing through my cds

giggle
i grab you

pull you over
kiss you hard on the small of your back

this is worth a thousand deaths

black

twisted by obsession
warped by excess
our hero hangs his head

beautiful young girls dance half nude
for your pleasure

spirits flow from the tap into my loins

beg for a reprieve
around every corner

black

phone as fear

all the clinics
all the jails
all the injury
time passes

all the women
all the heartbreak
all the tears
time passes

all the things i never did
all the words i never said
all the mistakes i'll make again
time passes

words come and go
as do people, jobs, friends, cars and lovers
my heart takes a beating and still hasn't failed me
but i have failed myself and probably will again

all the music that has flowed through
all the money earned and spent
all the bills paid and otherwise
time still passes

the love god

suck
fuck
eat
sniff
drink
smoke
die

is that all?

soundtracks

the passion is there
the method perfect
music i hear is never the music that is playing

come
for just a little while
listen with me

soft strings swirl in the air
like the smoke that billows from the end of your cigarette
pray it will never end

i'm blessed and cursed by having known you even
for those few drunken hours

come listen to our songs
pray it will never end, never end

chayne
for Jack, Gary, Johnathan and Dave

cutting heads with reckless abandon
we were in the wilds of untamed america
spirit and need triumph over the aloof
who always choose the sensible

don't collar us with your jive
we write, play and sing these songs because we have to
not always because we want to
i refuse to take responsibility for my ferocious
appetite for self-indulgence

purse

i wanna be her purse
always held close
holding all her secrets
her never leaving the house without me

sitting on the bed and watching as she gets dressed
this is truly magical

oh yes, to be her purse
holding her most valuable things and vitals
she would no doubt blow a fuse if she were to misplace me
but i keep in mind
she probably has a different purse for every day of the week
and still others for different outfits

ouch man

quack

ducks, geese and gulls
old people feed them
drunks and children feed them
madhouses let the population out for the sole
purpose
of feeding
ducks, geese and gulls

duck fuck
they don't quack
they laugh
they are free
and they are fed by people with souls bigger
than intelligence
hearts and spirits greater than reason

me

anger
distress
black, gray
even still more anger
misguided animosity
a fierce drive to be remote
why?

i'll never be clean again
running
hiding
hating
existing, never living
and one day closer to death

the witch in apartment one

what a pair we are
or were
two manipulating lowlifes of the highest order
you could manipulate the balls off a bulldog
and i would love to watch

i went to our local shithole today
someone asked where my woman was
that was very scary

even for me

santa

working on a drunk
playing one to the next
guitar sings out for help
piano just lays in my guts

you are on my mind
light and sweet
i crave to be near you
you're out there right now
being someone's spark
that brings me comfort

we are together
in spirits of the human condition
i'm getting soft
or i have always been soft
dough boy
that's me

now i'm thin and weak from life
i'm wasting away daily
bottle or not
christ was born on christmas day
to take me to the promised land
but not this year
only beer, retail and bitterness remain

5:21 a.m.

oh, your mouth
take my cum
yes, let's fuck and suck each other to tears
it's better than loving each other to death

game

death won't come
so i take back what i said

i believe i haven't any choice
i continue to work out my earthy living skills
i never will
love
fuck
or die on my terms

i shake
i'm shaking
i'll always shake
dent the car i lose my hearing and judgment

i'm horny for death – the ultimate lay
real sleep will never come again

i got impatient and bought a ticket for what i believe
 will be the only true solace in this game

the mourning chorus

birds fuck you when you sing
all you do is remind me it's mourning
and i am still alive

christmas '88

i got many presents
i am not in jail
i am not in a hospital
i am home and i am going to get drunk
if that is possible

tonight

this night should last forever
cool crisp breeze
fresh air through the trees

there is a sense of mischief all around
anything seems possible tonight

she holds him close and says, "i love you"
he closes his eyes and wishes he could die
right there in her embrace

he can never feel the way he feels tonight again
this night almost feels like hope
he could never sleep this night away
the stars intoxicate them both
he feels fresh for the first time in years
he believes in love

tonight
he wants to live a thousand lives
tonight
savor every moment

the next one is not promised to us
all he has is tonight
that seems like enough
he feels light

tonight
his heart is floating
catching the breeze
breathing you, the night, in deeply
feeling eternal as he exhales his hopes

into tonight

soup
Lenny Bruce 1925-1966

wop bastard
dago fuck
jew bag whore
wicked irish cunt
welcome
kraut fucker
spade shit and nigger white
welcome
spic tramp and cocksucker catholic
welcome
we are all in this together

we are all in the broth

home is where the war is

home is where the war is
i feel it in my guts and the palms of my hands
a stench lingers that smothers
good judgment

it's the human condition to grab whatever feels right at the time
we'll pay the price later

i continue to chip away at the place that is somewhere
in the middle

i will someday achieve it or die trying
marching on is what makes the journey

studying the past at too great detail
assures more failures

so it's onward
in a bevy of triumphs and failures
home is where the war is
the home of my heart is a constant battle-ground
heart and mind searching for the right mix

she's 17

this girl has fire
in her walk
in her eyes
she floors me

these are the ones that get you in the
place you didn't even know you had

when they slip away it truly is a tragedy
you get the certain feeling you'll never meet another
with that same fire

you're correct
every man has these women come and go in his life
they are as rare as those moments that pass
where you feel like you're complete

these ladies are the ones, my friends, you have to act on
because you will feel the loss every day of your life
certainly until the next fire comes along

sink

there truly is nothing better than sinking a few
on a cold, rainy afternoon
and staring off into the abyss
i wonder how many of us are death gazing this afternoon

just another drunk

in the grand scheme of things i'm just another drunk
so just step over me
don't kick me, beat me or hurt me
i'm doing that just fine myself

she works it

heather was wicked irish
i liked that
she won't budge

what a great game
ounce for ounce
the best in her league
i wanted that shit in my life
now she is fucking the produce man
god bless that poor fucker

no effect

i drink
i drink
and i drink
i'm bored to tears
why?
why doesn't the bottle work today?

the 80's

shitting what looks to be my colon into the toilet
no fun

turning my stomach into wet tissue paper
no fun

having an ass that bleeds like a virgin

no fun

the phone

ring you fuck
a line to the other unfortunate bastards
we are all in this together
we are all clowns
if you don't believe this
take a look into the mirror
you'll see the big red nose and rosy cheeks
laugh clown
all the way to your grave and never know it

new year's day

i sit and have nothing better to do than wonder

how many people died?

were beaten?

were mugged?

spent and raped?

were arrested for crimes they did or didn't commit?

on new year's day

funk

everywhere i go
and everyone i know
the funk follows
a hellish stink in my nostrils
sweating out my futility like a virus that has no end
and always fighting this losing battle

all of you

all of you unfortunates
you know who you are
i am with you in spirit

i sit behind this keyboard
and you sit in jail
you sit in flop houses
you sit in the streets
you sit in hospitals
you sit with people you hate
you sit with a lover
you sit in your own piss
you sit and bleed
on the inside as well as on the outside

i'm with you in spirit
i've been in all those places too
and i'll be back,
i promise

half hard

it's best when you are half hard
it's the ultimate play thing

it is even better when you haven't washed

like the bottle
the beginning is tedious
the end is dreadful
the in-between is glorious

half hard
that's what i crave

law against consistency

we live in a time
a time for everything that is proper
"you have been playing that damn music for hours.
give everyone a rest!" said the voice
"fuck them!" is my reply
they will get the rest of gods soon enough

hum

i hear the hum

it drives me mad

if that is still possible

desperate

desperate again
where is the glory?
where is the hope?
there is no solace for the desperate
only a desperate end

low

i had been drinking and watching the talent all afternoon.
then i decided to see her. she was great company with a load on.
the possibility of sex was always exciting. we never did fuck. we never
had any sex, come to think of it. maybe a brain fuck or two. she gave
great phone. she was crazy drunk on scotch when i arrived. the house
was complete shit but i said the mess didn't bother me. i suggested we
make a booze run, she had a totally different plan in mind. she wanted
to pick up a few bags of dope. i got an instant hard-on when i heard
this plan. you know, the death hard-on. i knew a place close where we
could cop. there was no way i was driving to the bronx like she had
suggested. i almost shit on myself while we were driving.

we cop and race back to the apartment. in minutes the kitchen table
is covered with needles, cookers and all kinds of shit. cotton. she tore
open the bags and they were empty. there was a pregnant silence.
inside i felt a great relief. she, however, did not share this feeling with
me. she was hell bent on getting off. i offered more booze and food to
pacify the beast. it only seemed to make things worse.

two hours and a lot of drinks later she dives on my lap, rubs my crotch
and says, "take us to the bronx baby and everything will be beautiful!"
it was at this very moment that I felt all the pain of the last 10 years.
i yelled repeatedly, "no bronx, no fucking bronx!"

i was getting a nasty taste of myself and i didn't like it. as i said earlier we never got physical. now she was licking my neck and grabbing my cock begging for dope. i said it would be best if i left, but the scotch had other plans.

she asked me to take her to the market for a few things. "this," i said, "i would gladly do." as shop-rite grew near things changed. if i didn't take her to the bronx she said she would throw a fit. i said watching you throw a fit in the parking lot would bring me great pleasure. "it's home or i am throwing you out of the fucking car right here on the pavement!" at this point i am very drunk and very angry.

i bring her back home and her lover is just pulling up as we arrive. she grabs my fucking car keys and runs screaming to the apartment. her lover and i follow as i try to explain to the poor bastard what's going on. he tries to reason with her but the bottle is really kicking. she refuses to give me back my car keys. he dives on her and starts to strangle her. i start to scream that this is not necessary and dive on the two of them. all in a quest for my car keys. they are both bleeding and we are all screaming at the top of our alcoholic lungs. i thought for sure someone would be leaving on a stretcher and no fucking way it was going to be me! not twice in one month! this went on for what seemed like hours and finally loverman got my keys and i tore off shaking and laughing out loud. i stuck a beer in my jacket pocket for the ride home and realized just how low i truly am.

and ashely also

why is it you remember me?
weeks can come and go
you still greet me with a smile
and more fire than any show girl in this world
you are dripping sexuality with every move
i've seen bastards give you their entire billfold
credit cards, identification, pictures of the family
i have never given you much

regardless
you treat me as if we shared something
i can only imagine what that could be
are there a handful of cats who just happen to fall
in your good graces?

i am truly charmed
and raging
and now there is a new reason
a new reason to write
and ashely also

remedy

i have grown very tired of running
it is an around the clock job
i am sure it would take much less energy to lay up

i really don't believe the lie
i don't think i ever did
it just sounded right in the beginning
nobody thinks about it until you're in too deep
that's the bitch about it
you're drowning
and you don't even remember falling overboard

you and what army?

it takes a lot of shit
to make a shit house pie
and i have eaten many
but there is always
always room for more
today however, i am stuffed

the drunk suffering artist act

it most certainly is wearing thin
i have little interest in self control
my heart cleansed in white wine and lies
and i don't want your world
i drink the spirit of indecision and sing your bedtime story

the incredible super elastic bubble plastic spastic boy

b-movie motherfucker
die with no grace
you are killing the joke

mommy, take me to the circus
we are living in one, my little shit

i have fucked in a way that is truly admirable
alone
myself
maybe i will just linger
time just keeps raping us

bone merchant

same game
same results
dismal failure, with no point of reference
bones are buried
along with the remains of light
what is the best possible outcome
stoned
best case scenario
binge, purge and die

sunshine on my side o the block

all drunks go to heaven
there is no true solace for the proud

rain of fire and saints
jesus forgive me

i am slipping away from nowhere
please save me from a fate worse than complacency

i love to blend in-between the cracks of your reality

shitface mofo

each day i die a little
this is what the almighty's plan is
so why fight it?

in love with the bottle and words
i can't seem to replace the bottle with anything

the bottle lies and drags me down lower than i ever imagined possible

this still does not change my love for not feeling the ground beneath my feet

detox kid

laying on the floor sweating and freezing
i'll have another drink, thank you very much
torn up in a love/hate battle
and feeling hopeless and never helpless

why do i not have control?
or better yet, why can't i give up the flight altogether?

to put it as simple as pie, i just love to be drunk

repetition

samey, samey
no new tales to tell
as a writer i am boorish at best

booze, booze, booze, booze
drugs, drugs, drugs, drugs
that's all folks

pain and suffering
killing my lifelines
and then writing about the grief

one more sleepless night

lay awake and watch the clock
my brain will not shut down
obsessed with all the hate in the world
feeling as much pain as i can muster up from memory

when can i write something that is not about suffering?
when I choose to stop suffering i would imagine

never look back and never worry about later
try this moment on for size

one size fits all

smother

overwhelmed by an endless tirade of images
what next?

i lay here with cock in hand
staring at the clock
feeling like there are so many games left to play
i can never do enough for the sake of the muses
this will be my fate

a puppet of words, sounds and images
keep breathing the night air in like a mouthful of sparks
wrapping my lips around my brain in an effort to shut down

i will ease my weary bones into sleep
dream of all of you who lay in completeness
i can never be anything other than what i am
a fool for words, sounds and images

loony tune

i am empty in the wake of a new day that will dawn
abusing my stomach with poisons
balance is my one true goal
i am the original all or nothing man

can this change
omni-positive
perhaps it already is happening
i just haven't caught up with it yet

the importance of doing it my way, will keep me free
i am a cripple for lust and flesh seeking
feast of wanton lovers in the dark
we strut and grin
i will always seek to be altered
balance again will laugh with me and at me

stir crazy

in the wake of another storm
dragging on the coat tails of a lesser success story
i wait in the dark
holding down the fort of diamonds and apathy

we wait
we wait

life is a series of waiting periods

when do we live?
when do we live?

the attack of the high class drunks

sipping and nibbling on only the best
they sit
chit chat
ignite each other's cigarettes with lighters that have
their initials inscribed on them
thumb their noses at the downtrodden and throw
money at charities that aim to help the needy

"but what about my needs?" the wiseass young rich man
asked in a loud voice

"i hate my parents and my cousin is fucking my wife!"

someone once told me that nobody suffers like the poor
i never believed this
no, my friends
pain and suffering are truly everywhere
they are probably the only things in this life
that will never discriminate

the plight of american white trash

there are those that will never handle the burden
of living regarding human concerns

food stamps, welfare
or six figure bank accounts
will not be the issue
it is a question of class

the animal instincts are fierce among the seedy
but after all is revealed
we all share very basic needs
the hunger to love and be loved
to suffer as little as possible
and the instinct to survive

we all just chose different means to an end,
an end i have come to believe has little significance
the journey is far more important than the destination

escape from the low life country

it was a sunny warm march afternoon
those that were now low on the food chain gathered around to
share bottles, pills and sorrow

i sat waiting for the bus
knowing full well i was a potential casualty

it wasn't a roll of the dice like i once subscribed to
it was a conscious decision
potential is wickedly misunderstood
it can take you where you didn't plan to go
the elevator goes...
up
down
or stops
somewhere in-between

the brothers grim

tangled
dragging ass
the whole town looking on as if i was the solitary cause of
all injustices plaguing our fair city
but i appeal to you my friends
i have been wronged
but once you hang
it is so very easy to put the noose back around your lifeless-
broken neck

oh, there is the rub
keep the downtrodden down
it cuts back on your taxes in the long run

drop dead perfect

all you need is cash
a good lawyer
a good mechanic
a good doctor
and a fantastic lay

girl (*like a drug*)

it's in her walk'
it's in her words
it's in her talk
it's in her curves

it's all her world
it's what she says
and what she doesn't

what she do and what she does
this girl is death's antidote
she makes me want to live forever

smiles, frowns, laughs and giggles
an acute sense of self
the sum of her parts is female
paradigm righteousness

i digress to childhood
summer crush and the first girl i kissed
goose bumps and butterflies in the stomach
i want her to be my lover, friend, mother and big sister

my mistress and nemesis
all in one affectation
please don't find me out
i lose my constitution when you are near
you could destroy me if you choose
i would rather be crushed than break the spell

the day after they put you in the ground

it rained
the day after they put you in the ground

i felt as lost as ever
the day after they put you in the ground

this life is not for me
i turned out all wrong

all the success in this world
won't change the emptiness

marked drowsiness
and writer's block

the day after they put you in the ground
throwing up my lines

and omnipresent hate for all
the day after they put you in the ground

always a new story to tell

i just got a dose of real crisp night air
fuck all if it didn't make me want to see another day

you, the girl from the club
or the boys in the band, what a twisted and beautiful lot

a new home
another movie
new friends
more drunks
better highs
deeper lows
a sense of thanking the maker i didn't open my wrists
not yet

let life fuck me senseless
life will take my life
not me,
i'll be too busy writing all this madness down
and, oh yes, more music

always more music

elapse

the passing of time is a reality that i just can't grasp
when is now?
moments pass
moments are forthcoming
when is the present?

i want to live, not exist

the zero man

wandering about, bouncing from here and there
i think of all the women in the world
breathe them in
loneliness haunts me
i am disenfranchised
always looking for a fresh start or a new angle
and a new angel
you, the girl from the bank
so fine

somehow the memory of women i've known
can never justify the longing for the ones
i'll never know

with one look you become a demi-god
but you'll crush me somehow
i promise i will force your hand
so for now i will look the other way

cold beer and lottery

you are tearing me apart
i say move over

we are all consumers
love and hate and a lot of gray in-between

we take and we take and we take some more
L.A. fuck you in the sunshine

N.Y. rain on my parade
it is rock and roll, tits and ass or beer and wine

film draws no boundaries

pain killer whore that took my soul
the joke's on you
there is no one home but us

bozos

here and now

a spark at the end of my tunnel
someone has made my heart a little lighter

a girl
a girl who is more alive than a hundred girls
she intoxicates me with beauty and honesty
relentlessly she can entice and fascinate me
never would i want her to compromise or change

should i fall from grace
i will always have the warmth and tenderness
she gave freely
she makes me believe in the power of the here and now
grateful for whatever moments i spent with her
in her eyes there is both a child and a woman
wise beyond her years

i feel selfless when i think of her
wanting only less pain and suffering in this world
and as if by some magic spell
this life truly seems a little more tolerable

her words and essence
a healing ointment for the blackness that festers all around
making me feel, somehow, all the madness is worthwhile

here and now

burn in mediocrity

momma said beware
momma said watch your step
momma said don't take the dare
now i know what momma meant

fools stay in a twist
fools always fall
fools can't resist
a fool's options are small

for every tear momma shed
my heart beats a little slower
you were the only selfless one i ever hurt
forgive me
let our souls rest in peace
i love you momma

flower man

three nights running for the flower man
30-foot face yelling
over a sea of woodstock babies
may i die now?

no, there are still more tales to tell
absorbed by press and the lack of press

life just keeps me dancing
up-down-all around
i am in the spin cycle
an amazing one has fueled new blood in my veins
i die to you, and for you
i eat my own
come to me
anytime

i dare you to mind fuck me senseless
i love knowing you are out there
bring me to your alter
i will bleed rivers for you and your new religion
give me your words
your flesh
your soul

i bone for a suck on your brain
your voice sends a fever to my funny boner
take me to your palace
i will be the peasant servant
just for a taste of your nectar
you're so yummy

comet girl

pass through my life
like a healing lady comet
so fast and shimmering

leave me feeling complete,
whole, alive for the moment

where are you now?
touching others

will you heal yourself?
abhorrent the notion
you may self destruct
on clear nights

i stare into the abyss
knowing that you are out there somewhere
now you are someone else's comet
this elucidates my darkened heart

i know you rage
i rage too
so rage
stop
and stay
stay and mend the wounds
this world desperately needs you
i need you
more than you can ever know

one more from the top

drained, desperate and disparaged
dispassionate with despair
disenfranchised and disillusioned
deluded, deranged and disassociated
disconnected and dilapidated
destroyed and demented
disastrously diabolic
disarray and disarranged
and a hole for a heart

fleeting moment

in one fleeting moment of clarity i deduced that
happiness and sadness are transient states of being
to chase one and exhume the other is futile at best
total wellness of being is all you can shoot for in this life
the shit will always hit the fan, it's just a house of cards

3 hours at the saint marks hotel

how did this happen?
again
from park ave. to park bench
from toast of the town
to begging for change
so long sanity, health, peace of mind
mangled once again
enduring the loss
broke
broken
surrendering to god

pray for deliverance and the reprieve that a new day can bring

steadfast and true

prayer doesn't promise any dispensation from self will
it offers only an anchor to solace
serenity can be found when you completely accept
the human condition

perfection is the enemy
progress is the goal

i am, by nature, self absorbed
spirit, mind and body in a constant search for balance

all roads in this life leading back to christ

eyebrows

stunning
she was the most
in all ways and forever
a voice to die for
eyes like a wild animal
one look and i knew why i drank
out of fear of loving, losing and living

the contemporary poet has-been

fuck the rich
eat the poor
write till there are no more holidays or words
28 is a motherfucker
just like all the rest
we sit and eat shit, but not me
i have words for breakfast

sex

nasty bastard as you think of all the decadence
you can dream up
umh! make it really stink
ingest all the filth and beauty in this world

what is real?
the bottle
i am totally empty and i am happy for that

if you don't believe me
check my bowels

bent over

ah, my first shave since i left the ward
not bad
haircut growing in nicely
now, with my head between my knees
i am shitting out everything i ever consumed,
or consumed me

two hours and still counting
i am sure there is an open safety pin in my stomach
out come all of you
heather
dad
b-movies
every song i ever composed or played
mom
every poem i ever wrote
poet goddess who i can't seem to touch

kevin, the one remains
frank and bobby who put me away

the pain has brought me to tears
now i laugh
as even more of this twisted life comes out
head still between my knees
i stop writing

about the author

(Photo by *Tom Zanca*)

Scott Henry Schiaffo was born in Passaic, New Jersey and is an actor/musician who plays guitar, keyboards, bass and harmonica.

He is best known to independent film fans as the *Chewlies Gum Guy* from *Kevin Smith*'s 1994 independent classic film, "Clerks." He's appeared in films alongside *Michael DeLorenzo* in "The Garden State" and *Selma Blair* in "The Broccoli Theory." He was featured in the *View Askew/Lions Gate* film "Vulgar" with *Brian O'Halloran* and *Ethan Suplee*.

Scott played the lead in "Idiots Are Us" which won Best Comedy Feature at the 2007 *New York International Independent Film and Video Festival*.

In 2011 Scott appeared in *Tom Zanca's* "Echoes & Voices" and in *Michael P. Russin's* Film "Don't Shoot." The latter won Best Low Budget Short at the 2011 *Jersey Shore Film Festival*.

Scott is currently a graduate student in the Professional Counseling Program at William Paterson University.

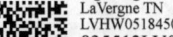
www.ingramcontent.com/pod-product-compliance
Lightning Source LLC
LaVergne TN
LVHW051845080426
835512LV00018B/3075